20th Century
PERSPECTIVES

The
Vietnam War

Douglas Willoughby

Heinemann Library
Chicago, Illinois

© 2001 Reed Educational & Professional Publishing
Published by Heinemann Library,
an imprint of Reed Educational & Professional Publishing,
Chicago, IL

Customer Service 888-454-2279

Visit our website at www.heinemannlibrary.com

Designed by AMR
Illustrated by Art Construction and Chris Brown (Pennant Illustration Agency)
Originated by Dot Gradations
Printed by Wing King Tong in Hong Kong.

Library of Congress Cataloging-in-Publication Data
Willoughby, Douglas.
    The Vietnam War / Douglas Willoughby.
        p. cm. -- (20th century perspectives)
    Includes index.
    ISBN 1-57572-439-1 (library binding)
    1. Vietnam Conflict, 1961-1975--Juvenile literature. I. Title. II. Series.

DS557.6.W55 2001
959.704'3--dc21

00-063238

Acknowledgments
The publishers would like to thank the following for permission to reproduce photographs:
Associated Press, pp. 30, 31; Bettmann/Corbis, pp. 36, 37; Corbis, pp. 13, 15, 27, 43; Corbis/Peter Turnley, p. 39; Corbis/Wally McNamamee, p. 42; Corbis/Bettman, pp. 5, 6, 8, 21; Corbis/Everett, p. 41; Corbis/Tim Page, p. 17; Hulton Getty, pp. 7, 9, 11, 12, 14, 18, 19, 20, 22, 28, 32, 34, 35, 43; Katz, pp. 24, 25; Magnum/Marc Ribould, p. 27; Network, p. 38, Peter Newark, p. 33; Rex Features, p. 40.

Cover photograph reproduced with permission of Corbis.

Special thanks to Mark Adamic for his help in the preparation of this book.

Some words are shown in bold, **like this.** You can find out what they mean by looking in the glossary.

Contents

The Vietnam War–An Overview

Today, Vietnam is a united country. It is about 992 miles (1,600 kilometers) long and covers an area a bit bigger than Italy. To the north is China, with Laos and Cambodia to the west. The South China Sea lies to the east. More than seventy-seven million people live in Vietnam, many along the Red River in the north, or in the delta of the Mekong River in the south. Some live in large cities like the capital, Hanoi, or Ho Chi Minh City, formerly Saigon. Many more are peasants, farming land that has been cleared from tropical forests. Between May and September, the monsoon rains fall and the water is used to grow rice, the main crop and the basic diet of the people. Along the coastal area, fishing and shipping are important sources of employment, but farming remains the main occupation.

This map shows modern Vietnam.

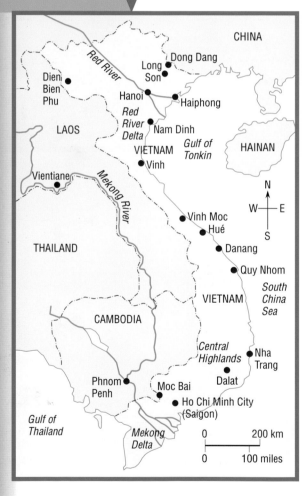

One of the longest wars in modern history

Vietnam has not always been a united country. In 1954, it was divided between North and South. From 1962 until 1975 it was the location of one of the longest wars in modern history, the Vietnam War. This war was a **civil war** between **communist** North Vietnam supported by China and the Soviet Union, and "free" South Vietnam backed mainly by the United States. During the thirteen years of the conflict, about 2.8 million U.S. soldiers found themselves fighting the North Vietnamese Army **(NVA)** and a communist guerrilla army (the **Vietcong**) in the jungles of Vietnam. More than 58,000 U.S. soldiers were killed and 304,000 wounded. The Americans were joined in the war by around 50,000 Australians, of whom 500 were killed, and a small group of New Zealanders, of whom 39 lost their lives. Sixty-eight U.S. women were killed; including nurses, aid workers, and missionaries.

Vietnamese suffering

The Americans, Australians, and New Zealanders and their communist enemy, the North Vietnamese Army and the Vietcong, who fought in the war, all suffered tragic losses of life. The main sufferers, however, were the common people of Vietnam. In the three years beginning in February 1965, the Americans dropped 1.1 million tons (1 million tonnes) of bombs on North Vietnam. They followed this with a program of chemical warfare. They also used deadly **napalm** that killed many civilians. By the time the war ended, many of their farms were destroyed, their land polluted by chemicals and as many as a million of them, for a variety of reasons, had become **refugees.**

These U.S. soldiers are passing a burning Vietnamese village.

The war and the media

The Vietnam War was the first war to be intensively covered by television cameras as well as by newspaper reporters. Modern technology brought the war into the homes of people throughout the world. For many Americans, seeing their young men fighting, suffering, and dying in the Vietnamese jungles was a shocking experience. Support for the war, which had been so strong at the beginning, changed to opposition. Enthusiasm turned to hostility. Many joined protest movements demanding an end to the war and the return of the thousands of young Americans fighting in it. Above all, many Americans began to ask questions such as "What are we doing there"? and "How did we get involved"?

The end at last

On March 29, 1973 the last U.S. troops left Vietnam. Many who survived the conflict are still suffering the physical and psychological effects of their experiences in the war. On April 30, 1975, the communist North Vietnamese Army and the Vietcong army marched into Saigon, the capital of the south and occupied it. Soon afterwards, Vietnam was united once again, but this time under communist rule. This invasion was in direct violation of the Paris peace accord. For those Americans who had fought in Vietnam, news of the fall of Saigon must have been particularly painful and many must have asked "What was the point of it all"? "For what purpose did so many of us die"? Although in recent years those who fought and died in Vietnam have been given fitting memorials, those same questions continue to be asked and the answers still remain difficult to hear.

The Background

From 111 B.C. until independence in A.D. 938, Vietnam was part of the Chinese empire. This long period of Chinese rule left its mark on the Vietnamese language, its religion, and its architecture. The Vietnamese were strongly Buddhist. In the 17th century, French Christian missionaries arrived. At first they received a friendly welcome, but this changed to hostility when they began converting the people to Catholicism. This became so disruptive that, in 1857, French soldiers were sent to protect the Catholic community. This was the first time that the French government became involved in Vietnam and it gave them an excuse to expand their overseas empire. Hostility continued. In 1858, the French Emperor, Napoleon III, sent 14 ships and 2,500 troops to the port of Tourane—now Danang. Fighting continued until 1868 when the Vietnamese emperor surrendered and made a peace treaty with France. In 1885, the Chinese signed an agreement accepting French control over Vietnam. In 1893, the French added Laos and Cambodia to their empire which, together with Vietnam, became known as French Indochina.

In 1858, Emperor Napoleon III of France sent troops to Vietnam to establish French control.

A French colony

Vietnam had valuable natural resources. By the turn of the century, the French were taking advantage of everything that her new colony had to offer. Large amounts of coal, tin, zinc, and rubber were being sent to France, and Vietnam was becoming a market for French manufactured goods. By 1938, 57 percent of all of Vietnam's imports were produced by French firms. To fully exploit these benefits, the French increased their control over the country. They built a system of roads, canals, and railways to transport raw materials and finished goods.

When it came to governing the colony, the highest officials were French, but at the middle and lower levels, the French made use of the Vietnamese. Many of these had become Catholics and had learned to speak French in French schools. Some of these pro-French Vietnamese became rich and powerful, but for the peasants and common Vietnamese life remained hard. The people paid taxes to the French to meet the cost of developing the country. Those who were unable to pay these taxes had to sell their land and work in the mines or on rubber plantations. The protests that followed were put down by force. Some of the protest leaders decided to leave the country rather than risk death. One of these was Ho Chi Minh, who was to become the leader of the movement for Vietnamese independence.

Ho Chi Minh and Vietnamese communism

Ho Chi Minh, also known as Nguyen Ai Quoc (Nguyen the Patriot), was born in 1890 and died in 1969. His father lost his job as a teacher when he refused to learn French. He spent his time helping the peasants and taught his family to believe in the importance of resisting the French. Ho's sister received a sentence of life imprisonment for stealing weapons from the French while working for them. Ho attended a grammar school and became a schoolteacher. Shortly afterwards, he left Vietnam. By 1914, Ho was working in the kitchens of a London hotel and in 1917 he arrived in Paris, where he studied the writings of Karl Marx and became a communist. He helped to found the French Communist Party in December 1920, and in 1925 set up the Revolutionary Youth League of Vietnam, followed by the Vietnamese Communist Party in 1930, and the Revolutionary League for the Independence of Vietnam in 1941.

Communism–the answer to Vietnam's problems

Perhaps Ho's most important experience came in 1924 when he visited the Soviet Union. The country was becoming **communist** after the 1917 revolution and Ho was very impressed by what he saw. He believed that communism was the answer to the problems of poverty facing the Vietnamese peasants. The land, owned by a few rich landowners, must be taken from them and given to the peasants. For this to be achieved, there would have to be a violent revolution. The French would be thrown out and the communists would take control of the country. If this was to happen, the peasants must be organized and trained. This was the job of the Communist Party which he would lead. For Ho, communism and Vietnamese freedom went together. However, he knew that if he returned to Vietnam, he would be imprisoned. So he settled in China, close to the Vietnam border. Here he set up the "Vietnam Revolutionary League," which, he hoped, would eventually lead the revolution.

Ho Chi Minh 1890–1969, was the communist leader of the North Vietnamese.

From World War II to Dien Bien Phu

When the new Vietnamese Republic was set up in 1976, Giap became Vice Premier.

The Japanese invade

In September 1940, as part of their plan for territorial expansion, the Japanese invaded Vietnam. The French surrendered and Ho saw the opportunity he had been waiting for. He returned to Vietnam in February 1941 and formed the **Vietminh** army. Led by General Giap, they began a **guerrilla war** in the jungle against the Japanese, using weapons supplied by the Soviet Union and the United States, who declared war on Japan in December 1941. In August 1945, following the dropping of atomic bombs on Japan by the United States, the Japanese surrendered and Ho thought that Vietnam was now free. After all, the French were gone and the Japanese had been defeated, albeit with American, French, British, and Russian help. Surely the independence of the Vietnamese people would be recognized.

In September 1945, therefore, he announced the creation of the Democratic Republic of Vietnam. This was what he had dreamed of and worked for over many years. After the war ended until 1946, Vietnam was occupied by China and Britain. Ho believed that it was only a matter of time before they handed over power to him.

General Giap

Vo Nguyen Giap was born in 1912. As a student, he became a **communist** and joined Ho Chi Minh's Revolutionary Youth League of Vietnam in 1926. In 1939, Giap fled to China to avoid arrest by the French, but his sister-in-law was executed and his wife died in a French prison. From 1941 to 1945, Giap was Ho's assistant in the guerrilla war against the Japanese. He commanded the Vietminh against the French between 1946 and 1954. The victory at Dien Bien Phu was his greatest triumph. He remained Commander-in-Chief of the Vietminh throughout the Vietnam War until 1975. When the new Vietnamese Republic was set up in 1976, Giap became Vice-Premier.

The French return

Ho was therefore angry when, in 1946, Vietnam was returned to the French, who refused to accept the Democratic Republic of Vietnam. Ho and the Vietminh now found themselves fighting yet another war, this time against the French. After early setbacks, the Vietminh began to win important victories, particularly after 1949, when the Chinese communists helped them. But, in 1953, victory seemed a long way off.

The French army dropped paratroopers over Dien Bien Phu in 1954. The French were defeated after a 56-day siege.

The French still controlled the south, supporting Bao Dai, the former emperor, as head of state. Ho realized, however, that the longer the war lasted, the greater were the chances of a Vietnamese victory. He also knew that in France, the people were tired of the fighting. Ninety thousand French troops had already been wounded or killed in a war lasting seven years. There was no sign of victory and the cost of the war was a great burden on French taxpayers. With declining support the French desperately needed to end the war with a victory. Their commander in Vietnam, General Navarre, hoped to achieve this in 1954 at Dien Bien Phu.

The Battle of Dien Bien Phu

To stop the Vietminh forces from returning to their bases in Laos, Navarre set up a defensive system at Dien Bien Phu. He knew that to reopen the route into Laos, the Vietminh would have to attack it. Instead, led by Giap, they surrounded it with thousands of troops and a vast system of well-constructed trenches. They maintained their siege for 56 days, during which time the attention of the whole world was focused on that French garrison and on what would happen to the besieged soldiers. For all those 56 days, they were subjected to a constant bombardment from siege guns placed in the hills over the French camp. On May 7, 1954, the siege came to an end. Around 2,000 French troops had been killed and more than 10,000 surrendered. Vietnamese losses were between 8,000 and 10,000 and bodies of soldiers from both sides remain buried in the defensive system, even today. The French suffered a humiliating defeat which meant the end of their control of Vietnam and Indochina. For Ho Chi Minh and for General Giap and the Vietminh, Dien Bien Phu was a great victory and would now surely lead to a united, free, and communist Vietnam. That is what Ho and his followers believed was about to happen.

The United States Gets Involved

This map shows the division of Vietnam after the Geneva Accords of 1954.

In April 1954, shortly before the French surrender at Dien Bien Phu, the foreign ministers of North and South Vietnam, Cambodia, Laos, China, the United States, the Soviet Union, Britain, and France met in Geneva, Switzerland, to try to reach a peaceful solution to the problems of Korea and French Indochina. The Geneva Accords, as they were known, were of great importance. They set the scene for the Vietnam War and speeded up American involvement.

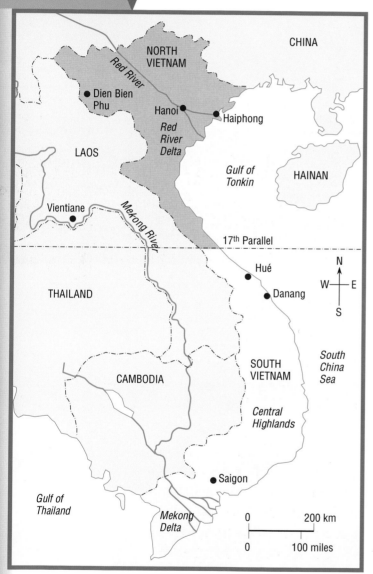

The Geneva Accords

- There was to be a cease-fire
- Vietnam would be divided at the 17th parallel of latitude.
- North Vietnam would be **communist** and ruled by Ho Chi Minh.
- South Vietnam would be ruled by Ngo Dinh Diem, a strong opponent of communism.
- French troops would leave Vietnam.
- The **Vietminh** would leave South Vietnam. Each side had 300 days to withdraw troops.
- The Vietnamese people could choose to live in the north or the south.
- By July 1956, a general election would be held throughout Vietnam for the people to decide the future of the country.

Although some of his supporters were angry that Vietnam was still not a united communist country after the defeat of the French, Ho Chi Minh was not worried. He knew that in the free elections the communists would win. Most Vietnamese were poor peasants who believed that their lives could only be improved if the communists took power and gave them land. In the United States, President Eisenhower had reached the same conclusion and suggested that if free elections were to be held, as many as 80 percent of the Vietnamese would vote communist. He decided that the United States must make sure that those elections never took place.

The Cold War begins

After World War II, the United States and the Soviet Union became the world's great superpowers, joined after the revolution in 1949 by communist China. The Soviet Union was communist and the United States **capitalist.** Neither trusted the other. Each believed the other country was trying to destroy it and the other countries it influenced. So, after 1945, the **Cold War** began. The Americans saw the Soviet Union as an evil threat which must be resisted. Speaking to Congress as early as March 1947, President Harry Truman had set out, in what became known as the Truman Doctrine, what the United States should do to stop communism from spreading. The Americans must help any country fighting communism by sending them money and weapons and, if necessary, soldiers to fight with them.

President Harry S. Truman (1945–1953) believed the United States should help any country fighting communism.

Closely connected to the Truman Doctrine was the **domino theory,** which stated that if communism took over one particular country then those nearest to it were immediately at risk and likely to fall next. A look at the map of Indochina will show clearly that this area was a perfect example of the domino theory in action. Many U.S. leaders believed that if Vietnam fell to communism, then Laos, Cambodia, and Thailand would immediately be threatened.

Eisenhower

Eisenhower became President in 1953. He continued Truman's policy. In the early years of his presidency, however, Eisenhower moved slowly. He realized that the U.S. people would not support sending troops to Vietnam, particularly since more than 50,000 U.S. soldiers had recently been killed fighting in Korea. Instead, he sent in a small group of advisers under Colonel Edward Lansdale, whose task was to use advertising, propaganda, and U.S. dollars to persuade the South Vietnamese people not to support the communists in the forthcoming elections. Instead, they should vote for Ngo Dinh Diem as president—the man backed by the U.S. government.

The United States Gets Pulled In

Ngo Dinh Diem

Ngo Dinh Diem, was president of South Vietnam from 1955 until his assassination in 1963.

Unlike the majority of Vietnamese, Ngo Dinh Diem was Catholic. He was educated by the French, worked for them as an administrator, and at the age of 25 became a provincial governor. Dinh Diem spent some of the French Indochina War, between 1946 and 1954, in the United States meeting influential Americans and convincing them that he should be a future leader of the South. So effective were his efforts that the United States nominated him as South Vietnamese president at Geneva in 1954. If the Americans backed Dinh Diem because they thought they could control him, they were mistaken. He often ignored their advice, but they kept up their support because there was no alternative.

In October, 1955, Dinh Diem was elected president of South Vietnam in elections which were violent and hardly fair. Shortly afterwards, he made a grave error. Having received a reminder from the North that under the Geneva Agreement, a general election for the whole of Vietnam was due in July 1956, he refused to accept the elections. As many as 100,000 people from a variety of political and religious groups protested, and then were imprisoned or killed. The Americans now found themselves supporting a president who was becoming increasingly unpopular with the people in a situation where violence was escalating.

NLF founded

Throughout Vietnam, **communist** supporters of Ho Chi Minh and many others were horrified at the refusal of Dinh Diem to hold a general election. Some resorted to violence, and in 1959, 1,200 government officials were murdered. Ho disliked this approach, and in 1960 brought all the different groups together as the "National Front for the Liberation of South Vietnam," the **NLF,** or "**Vietcong,**" as the United States called it. Their aim was to remove the Diem government by any means, including violence, and replace it with a government representing all the people of Vietnam. Just as important was their promise to the peasants that they would give them land. This promise made it certain that most of the peasants would support the Vietcong in the war which was about to begin. The NLF, or Vietcong, with Chinese and, if necessary, Russian support, were preparing to fight a war against the Diem government in the south, backed by the United States.

President John F. Kennedy and Vietnam

John F. Kennedy, who was elected U.S. president in 1960, was a strong believer in the Truman Doctrine and the **domino theory.** According to him, the United States would be willing to "pay any price, bear any burden, meet any hardship, support any friend, oppose any foe to assure the survival and success of liberty."

Kennedy was willing to continue U.S. involvement in Vietnam and to increase it if victory was a possibility. In 1961, he sent money to the South Vietnamese to increase their army from 150,000 to 170,000 soldiers, plus another 100 advisers to train them. This decision was kept from the U.S. public because it broke the Geneva Agreement. Between 1963 and 1973, the Americans were in Vietnam, fighting a **guerrilla war** mainly against the Vietcong. The Vietcong fought in small groups and used their knowledge of their own countryside to hide from the Americans and to pick the places where they wanted to fight.

John Fitzgerald Kennedy (1917–1963) was born in Brookline, Massachusetts. He was the second son of Joseph Kennedy (1888–1969), a rich banker and financier who served as U.S. ambassador to England between 1938 and 1940. John was educated at Choate School, Harvard University, and the London School of Economics. During World War II, he served as commander of a torpedo-boat in the South Pacific and was badly wounded. He entered politics when the war ended and served as a Democratic Congressman from 1946. In 1952, he was elected senator for Massachusetts.

In January 1961, he became the first Roman Catholic president in United States history and at the age of 43, the youngest elected president. He began his presidency with high ideals and the promise of a "new frontier" for the U.S. people; civil rights and a better life at home and more opportunities to serve underdeveloped countries abroad. In foreign affairs, he soon found himself with problems, particularly in 1962, when Soviet missiles were found in Cuba. He also increased U.S. involvement in Vietnam. On November 22, 1963, in Dallas, he was assassinated.

In his inaugural speech, Kennedy said "Americans would pay any price . . . to assure the survival and the success of liberty." This would be tested in Vietnam

The Vietcong and Guerrilla Warfare

Mao Zedong and guerrilla warfare

Mao Zedong had used guerrilla tactics when leading the **communist** revolution in China, which ended in victory in 1949. Ho Chi Minh and the **NLF** greatly admired Mao and decided to use the same tactics against the Americans and South Vietnamese army in Vietnam. They organized the guerrilla army into small groups of between three and ten soldiers, called cells. The cells worked together but had little knowledge of each other, so that if any were captured and tortured, they would not give away too much information.

Mao Zedong was the Chairman of the Chinese Communist Party of the People's Republic of China, 1949–1976.

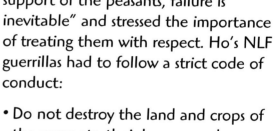

Peasant support

If the **Vietcong** guerrillas were going to win the war, they must have the support of the peasants. They needed food, shelter, and somewhere to hide when being hunted. Mao, like Ho, the leader of millions of peasants, believed that "without the constant and active support of the peasants, failure is inevitable" and stressed the importance of treating them with respect. Ho's NLF guerrillas had to follow a strict code of conduct:

- Do not destroy the land and crops of the peasants, their houses, and belongings.
- Do not force the peasants, against their wishes, to sell or lend you anything.
- You must always keep your word.
- Do not do or say anything which will lose the respect of the peasants.
- You must help the peasants in their daily work.

Guerrilla tactics

The NLF won the support of the peasants because they promised to take land from large landowners and give it to the peasants. The peasants were told that the Americans and South Vietnamese would take the land back. The peasants agreed they would feed, shelter, and hide the guerrillas in return for land. In some cases, the peasants actually became guerrillas and joined the war. The vast majority of peasants backed the guerrillas, but those who refused despite the code of conduct, were often threatened and beaten.

Using the peasant villages as their base, the guerrillas went out into the jungle. They attacked units of the South Vietnamese army, or **ARVN—**Army of the Republic of Vietnam—and ambushed patrols of U.S. soldiers. They then disappeared back into the jungle. They hid in the villages, in the houses, or in tunnels built for the sole purpose of hiding them and linked directly to the jungle. When the Americans arrived, there was no sign of the enemy. Against U.S. policy, some U.S. soldiers tortured the villagers to get information and sometimes burned their houses and crops. This angered the peasants even more and made them support the NLF.

These U.S. soldiers are carefully crossing a monkey bridge built of bamboo and vines.

Jungle tactics

In the jungle, the guerrillas never chose to fight unless they were certain of winning. They often attacked small enemy patrols, usually at night. Early in the war, they used simple daggers, and swords. Later, they were able to use better weapons, including explosives captured from the Americans. The U.S. soldiers suffered a terrible ordeal. The jungle they had to patrol was dense and the rice fields wet. The heat was often intense, the climate unfamiliar, and they were attacked by insects and leeches. There was also the threat of Vietcong booby traps, sharpened bamboo staves, mines, **grenades,** and artillery shells, waiting to be stepped on and set off. The guerrillas knew that the longer the war lasted, the greater their chance of victory. They knew that the Americans would give in before they did. After all, this was their home.

A U.S. marine captain described the problem: *You never knew who was the enemy and who was the friend. They all looked alike. They all dressed alike. They were all Vietnamese. Some of them were Vietcong . . . The enemy was all around you . . .*

The Ho Chi Minh Trail

For the **guerrilla war** to succeed, the **NLF** had to keep their guerrilla armies in the south equipped with fresh troops, supplies, and weapons. Many of these supplies and weapons came from **communist** China and the Soviet Union and the fresh troops came from North Vietnam. They all arrived in the south along the Ho Chi Minh trail. This was a collection of paths and routes through the jungle. **Vietcong** guerrillas traveled down the trail from the north to join the war in the south. The NLF received about 66 tons (60 tonnes) of supplies each day using the trail. They were carried by a variety of different methods, including trucks, oxen, and bicycles. Along the trail, there were camps where the guerrillas could rest and receive medical treatment.

This map details the route of the Ho Chi Minh trail through Laos, Cambodia, and finally into Vietnam.

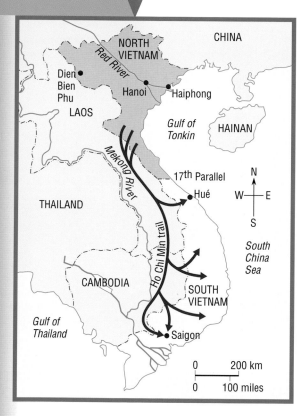

When the war began, it took as long as six months to travel down the trail from North Vietnam to Saigon. As the war continued, the trail became wider through increased use. By 1970, the journey was being completed in six weeks. The Ho Chi Minh trail was so vital to keeping the guerrillas supplied that the Americans tried to bomb it, but the jungle was so thick that they found it difficult to see it from their planes. To stop the trail from being used, the Americans did try to lay mines and barbed wire across it, but they abandoned this idea in 1967 when the Vietcong attacked the soldiers laying them. Electronic devices dropped to detect enemy movement were unsuccessful. They picked up everything that moved—including animals.

The Tet Offensive

The Vietcong spent most of their time fighting in the jungle, but at times they came out to attack the Americans directly. The Tet Offensive on January 31, 1968, was directed at targets throughout South Vietnam.

In September 1967, the NLF launched attacks on U.S. bases. The Americans were encouraged that, at last, the Vietcong appeared to have left the jungle and that, by the end of 1967, the Vietcong had lost 90,000 men. General Westmoreland, the commander of the U.S. forces, was sure that with such heavy enemy losses, a U.S. victory was now certain. But Westmoreland was unprepared. On January 31, 1968, during the Tet New Year festival, 70,000 North Vietnamese soldiers and Vietcong launched surprise attacks on 36 cities and towns throughout South Vietnam, thus breaking the holiday truce. It was now clear that the attacks on U.S. positions the previous September, had been intended to draw U.S. soldiers from the towns they were defending to prepare for the Tet Offensive.

The Americans were shocked by such well-organized attacks and by how easy it was for the NLF to attack so many towns and cities. What surprised them most was the way in which the Vietcong entered the grounds of the U.S. Embassy in Saigon. They did not capture the building, but killed five U.S. marines and took the main radio station. The Americans were also deeply worried that the NLF were able to find 70,000 new soldiers so soon, having lost 90,000 up to the end of 1967.

From a military viewpoint, it could be said that the Tet Offensive was an American victory. The U.S. lost 1,536 soldiers with 7,764 wounded, but 45,000 NLF soldiers were killed. What was most important, however, was that the U.S. people and politicians now realized that they were misled by Westmoreland and his military staff. Westmoreland had deliberately falsified reports to Lyndon Johnson, who became president in 1963 following Kennedy's assassination. Under the current war strategy, the United States could not win the Vietnam War. The NLF had vast numbers of soldiers. Coming into South Vietnam down the Ho Chi Minh trail; they would eventually overwhelm the Americans.

A wounded woman is carried away from the shelling as **refugees** *flee Saigon after a Vietcong attack.*

Lyndon Baines Johnson (1908–1973) was born in Stonewall, Texas, in 1908. He began his working life as a teacher and was elected to the U.S. House of Representatives as a Democrat in 1937. During World War II, he served as a naval officer while still a congressman. He was elected a senator for Texas in 1948 and became U.S. vice-president when Kennedy became president in 1961. Immediately after Kennedy's assassination in 1963, Johnson was sworn in as president and re-elected in 1964. At home, he introduced medical benefits for older people and civil rights laws. He became unpopular, however, because he increased U.S. involvement in Vietnam. As more and more U.S. soldiers died, he became increasingly disliked. He decided not to seek re-election to the presidency in 1968. He retired to his Texas ranch where he died in 1973.

U.S. Strategies and Tactics

This photo shows
U.S. soldiers with
two villagers from
a "safe village."

Strategic hamlets policy

The Americans used a variety of methods to fight the **Vietcong** in the jungles of Vietnam. The strategic hamlets, or safe villages, policy was introduced under President Kennedy from 1962. Its purpose was to isolate the Vietcong from the villages of South Vietnam and deprive them of the supplies and soldiers they needed. This was done by moving the villagers away from the Vietcong and placing them in new villages surrounded by barbed wire and guns. By September 1962, about a quarter of the South Vietnamese population was said to have been moved into safe villages. The policy failed. The peasants hated being moved from the villages that they and their ancestors had lived in for generations. They also hated having to leave their land and resented having to work building trenches to protect the villages. The policy became so unpopular that many peasants actually joined the Vietcong. The "Hearts and Minds" campaign tried to win the Vietnamese peasants over by attempting to persuade them that the Americans were on their side. This policy also failed.

Search and destroy

In 1965, General Westmoreland began a more direct "search and destroy" approach. Its purpose was simple: to find the Vietcong in the jungle and the villages and destroy them. U.S. soldiers patrolled through the jungle and into the villages to find guerrillas—a more difficult task than it sounds. It was often impossible for the Americans to tell the difference between the guerrillas and the peasants. They often killed innocent civilians by mistake.

Around villages controlled by the Vietcong, there were networks of tunnels in which the guerrillas could hide from U.S. and **ARVN** forces. They were built large enough for the guerrillas to hide in, but too small for the Americans to investigate.

Bombing North Vietnam

In March 1965, under "Operation Rolling Thunder," the United States began the bombing of North Vietnam. Its aim was to destroy the economy of the north and stop the support for the guerrillas in the south. The bombing was intended to last for eight weeks. In fact, it lasted eight years, in which time, eight million bombs were dropped. This was more than three times the number of bombs dropped in all of World War II. The United States took care to ensure that only military targets were bombed, but at times accidentally killed civilians. As a tactic, the bombing of military and industrial targets in North Vietnam failed because the north was mainly a farming country. Most importantly, the Chinese and Russians were able to replace all of the supplies and troops that U.S. bombing destroyed. Many U.S. military leaders thought that if the U.S. Navy and Air Force had been allowed to attack the key supply areas of Hanoi and Haiphong Harbor, as they wished, the war could have been won, or at least sent to a stalemate by the lack of supplies to the North. Politicians had stopped these plans because they did not want to see the war escalate because of any accidental killings of Soviet or Chinese "advisers."

NUMBERS OF U.S. TROOPS IN VIETNAM, 1962–1972	
YEAR	TOTAL
"ADVISERS"	
1962	12,000
1963	15,000
1964	23,310
GROUND TROOPS	
1965	184,310
1966	385,300
1967	485,600
1968	536,000
1969	484,330
1970	335,790
1971	158,120
1972	24,000

(SOURCE: STANTON'S *VIETNAM ORDER OF BATTLE*)

Ground troops

The **Gulf of Tonkin Resolution** in 1964 gave the president freedom to take action in Vietnam. The first U.S. troops to arrive in Vietnam, apart from advisers, were 3,500 Marines who landed on March 8, 1965. For the next three years, the number increased rapidly, reaching 536,000 by 1968. President Johnson was determined to fight **communism** in Vietnam by sending in more and more troops. U.S. troops stopped South Vietnam from collapsing but could not defeat the Vietcong. Although in early 1968, Johnson and many of his generals still believed that they were winning.

This U.S. B-52 bomber is dropping bombs on North Vietnam in "Operation Rolling Thunder."

Methods of Warfare

The Americans in Vietnam were able to draw on a vast arsenal of different types of weapons and associated technology:

- Helicopters were widely used by the United States. They were used to transport troops quickly, and at short notice. They were also used to remove soldiers from the jungle if the fighting became too difficult or if they were injured. Between 1965 and 1973, helicopters carried 406,022 injured U.S. soldiers to hospitals. While using helicopters may have had its benefits, it did mean that the Americans had even less direct contact with the peasants, essential to victory in such a **guerrilla war.**

- Throughout the war, the U.S. Seventh Fleet, made up of 125 ships and 64,000 men, controlled the seas around Vietnam. From their aircraft carriers, they sent fighter planes and bombers to attack the North. From offshore, battleships shelled **Vietcong** positions. They also tried to stop supplies from reaching the Vietcong from the sea by **blockading** the coast. Hundreds of ships were stopped and searched, but there were so many that some supplies slipped through.

- The Americans fighting in Vietnam made considerable use of **anti-personnel bombs.** Flechette bombs were filled with many small, metal darts. Canister rounds contained many small projectiles and were used against **NVA** and Vietcong troops. Plastic and metal needles, rather than metal pellets, were sometimes used in anti-personnel bombs. The advantage was that plastic could not be detected on X-rays.

U.S. aircraft flew in low to spray defoliants on the dense jungle growth.

- The great problem facing the Americans in Vietnam was actually finding the Vietcong in the thick, tropical jungle. For this reason, in 1962, President Kennedy approved "Operation Ranch Hand." This involved spraying chemicals over the jungle from aircraft to try to destroy the vegetation and reveal Vietcong hiding places. The chemical used was "**Agent Orange,**" which contained traces of the most toxic forms of **dioxin.** In 1969, 2,554,721 acres (1,034,300 hectares) of forest were destroyed.

` Not only did Agent Orange destroy thousands of trees, but it was later found to have caused birth defects in children. It also caused cancers in soldiers fighting in the war.

• Chemicals were also sprayed on crops. Between 1966 and 1969, the chemical "Agent Blue" was sprayed on 688,211 acres (278,610 hectares). The aim was to deprive the guerrillas of food. In fact, the ordinary peasants suffered most from the spraying. The spraying resulted in poor rice harvests and polluted land that the peasants and their ancestors had farmed for generations. The land remained unworkable for many years. Between 1962 and 1971, the Americans sprayed about 19,026,000 gallons (72 million litres) of **herbicide,** including more than 11,098,500 gallons (42 million litres) of Agent Orange, on the jungles of Vietnam to destroy the Vietcong's cover. Many U.S. soldiers claimed that the vegetation grew again quicker and thicker than before.

• As well as dropping explosive bombs and chemicals, U.S. forces also used bombs containing chemicals that caught fire. Of those used, **napalm** is the best known. Napalm is a mixture of gas and chemical thickener. It produces a tough sticky gel that attaches itself to the skin. The chemical within it, white phosphorus, burns for a considerable time. Although most napalm was dropped on military targets, photos of Vietnamese civilians, particularly children, burned by napalm, were seen throughout the world. These images did much to damage the reputation of the U.S. cause in Vietnam.

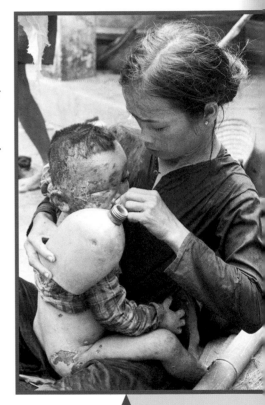

This Vietnamese mother is giving water to her child who is burned by napalm.

Vietnamese villagers as well as U.S. service personnel who came into contact with chemicals such as Agent Orange, continue to suffer from the effects of their exposure, more than three decades after the war.

I served as an Interpreter/Translator in I Corp 1963–1964. The majority of my work consisted of accompanying doctors into the field to provide medical help to villagers. During this period we were constantly exposed to Agent Orange. We were drenched with it, we bathed in it, and I'm sure we even drank the stuff. Shortly after my retirement in 1969, I came down with peripheral neuropathy (nerve damage) which has now progressed to the point to where it is very difficult to stand or walk without assistance.

U.S. Vietnam veteran, November 2000

U.S. Soldiers and the Vietnam War

During the course of the war, about 2.8 million U.S. soldiers served in Vietnam. At the beginning, they were professional soldiers who had made the army their career. They were well trained and committed. By 1967, however, most of the soldiers had been **drafted,** or forced to join. The average age of U.S. soldiers in Vietnam was nineteen, and their tour of duty lasted twelve months. About 60 percent of the soldiers were likely to see combat or be shot at. The others were employed in supplying the needs of the fighting troops, but could be fired on at any time by guerrillas. The average U.S. soldier had a two percent chance of being killed and a ten percent chance of being seriously wounded, but for those involved in the fighting, the casualty rate was of course far higher. Of those killed in the fighting, 43 percent died within the first three months. In total, about 58,000 U.S. service men and women were killed.

The draft

The U.S. Army drafted young American men at the age of eighteen. To reduce the stress on them, they served for just a year, which, it was hoped, would keep up morale. In fact, the only aim for many was to survive until their year was ended. When the young soldiers arrived in Vietnam, they were very often sent into units to replace men who had been killed or wounded. These replacements were often not accepted by the others in the unit because their inexperience might result in mistakes that could lead to loss of life. Not all young U.S. men were drafted. Those who were in college could have their draft delayed.

Patrols by U.S. troops in the dense forest areas of Vietnam were especially hazardous. Streams such as this one below were often booby trapped by the **Vietcong** *and peasants.*

Experiences of fighting

U.S. soldiers involved in the fighting often found themselves in small units patrolling the jungle in search of guerrillas. As well as being worried that they might be ambushed, they had to be on the look-out for booby traps, such as sharpened bamboo stakes hidden under sticks and leaves and **trip-wires** across jungle paths, which might set off **grenades.** They also had to be careful that they did not trigger a "Bouncing Betty" mine by standing on it and causing it to explode, injuring all around. The climate in the jungle was damp, hot, and humid, and heat exhaustion was common. Although it became cooler in the evening, soldiers then had to cope with **malarial** mosquitoes. They found it difficult to find the guerrillas in the thick tropical jungle and this made them even more frustrated.

Soldiers, officers, and ROE

Because many soldiers were serving in Vietnam for only a year, it was difficult to make each **platoon** an effective fighting unit. By the time many soldiers had become

This illustration shows three types of booby traps used by the Vietcong in Vietnam.

trained and fairly experienced, it was time to return home. Many also realized that because they were in Vietnam for only one year, their main aim must be to endure the year and get home alive. Their officers were different. They were professional career soldier, and many saw success in the war as the way to gain promotion. Sometimes, they were prepared to sustain heavy losses to achieve success.

In order to reduce the risks to the Vietnamese civilians, U.S. political leaders in Washington established strict Rules of Engagement (ROE) that U.S. soldiers, on the ground and in the air, were forced to follow. ROE were detailed instructions that dictated what tactics could and could not be used in fighting the enemy in South Vietnam, North Vietnam, Laos, and Cambodia. These ever-changing rules could be extremely complex and crazy. Yet they were rigidly enforced and careers were destroyed over perceived violations. The ROE further demoralized many soldiers because they increased the risk to U.S. forces and gave significant advantages to the enemy. Often, U.S. soldiers and pilots had to contact their headquarters to get permission to shoot at the enemy. Sometimes the permission came too late, if at all.

Declining Morale

The morale of U.S. soldiers was high at the beginning of the war. They were professionals who believed that they were fighting for the freedom of Vietnam. As the war continued, the deaths increased, and more men of common backgrounds, particularly African Americans, were **drafted** against their will. Morale began to decline. Many began to question what they were fighting for and whether they could actually win. Those directly involved in the fighting realized that the war was going badly and lost confidence in their officers. Some tried to desert, which means leaving their units without permission.

Drugs

As the morale of U.S. fighting troops fell and the boredom of those not directly involved grew, drug-taking increased. The best units in the U.S. Army and Marine Corps on the front lines had little use for troops who were under the influence. Most drugs were used by people far from the fighting and who had the opportunity to use drugs without much consequence. Field troops on leave or at base camp also used drugs. Many drugs were easily available and could be purchased cheaply throughout South Vietnam. Marijuana was the most popular, but cocaine and heroin were also used. The troops used **amphetamines** to keep themselves awake during night patrols. The problem was so bad that in 1971, 20,000 troops were treated for drug abuse. Drugs reduced the efficiency of U.S. soldiers, much to the delight of the **Vietcong.**

A photographer captured this picture of some of the victims of the My Lai massacre.

The Massacre at My Lai

On March 16, 1968, a **platoon** of U.S. soldiers approached the small village of My Lai, just south of Khe San. The platoon had already suffered heavy casualties from booby traps, snipers, and mines and were becoming frustrated that they could not find the Vietcong. The villagers were suspected of hiding guerrillas, but when the Americans arrived, they could find no trace of them. Under the command of Lieutenant William Calley, the company committed the worst recorded atrocity of the war. Later investigations revealed that several hundred men, women, children, and babies had been murdered.

Full details of the massacre were kept from the public. The official version was that 90 Vietcong fighters had been killed and one U.S. soldier shot in the foot. In November 1969, the full story broke. Americans were horrified by news of the massacre and that the news had been concealed for eighteen months. Calley was put on trial for murder, found guilty, and sentenced to life imprisonment. He served three and a half years before President Richard Nixon pardoned him.

The My Lai massacre divided U.S. public opinion. Many believed that the soldiers' actions were right because the villagers were hiding the Vietcong. Others were horrified. Some were angry that only Calley had been tried. Americans realized that their soldiers in Vietnam were under great stress and pressure and that at My Lai in March 1968, they had simply cracked. The massacre confirmed the feeling, growing since the Tet Offensive of 1967, that the Vietnam War was now a war which America could not win under the current strategy.

These villagers are survivors of the My Lai Massacre.

Personal accounts

Calley had a clear idea of what he had done.

The only crime that I have committed is in judgment of my values. Apparently, I valued my troops' lives more than I did that of the enemy.

Vietnam, Alan Pollock

A My Lai villager saw the massacre differently.

It's why I'm old before my time. I remember it all the time. I'm all alone and life is hard. Thinking about it has made me old . . . I won't forgive as long as I live—think of the babies being killed, then ask me why I hate them.

Four Hours at My Lai, Yorkshire Television

The Vietnamese People and the War

As early as 1954, Ho Chi Minh and the **communists** knew that Vietnam could only become independent and reunited by force. Only war could remove the armies that were occupying the country and preventing reunification. In the 1960s, the enemies were the Americans. To begin with, the communists used local **Vietminh** and **Vietcong** soldiers in the South, but later these were joined by soldiers from the North, who traveled down the Ho Chi Minh trail. Generally, the guerrillas really believed in the cause for which they were fighting. Their generals were prepared to accept heavy losses, knowing they could easily get fresh troops. The Americans knew all too well that, if large numbers of their troops died, the war would become very unpopular at home. The North Vietnamese were fighting for their own country and for them the war had a clear aim—victory and reunification.

The majority of the North Vietnamese people supported the war and their government. Support came also from the Soviet Union, which provided 8,000 anti-aircraft guns and 200 anti-aircraft launching sites for the North Vietnamese. While morale among the communists was far higher than among the Americans, the war was not easy for them either, and there were exceptions. One young Vietcong soldier writing to his girlfriend in 1971 said, *"This terrible war makes so many strange thoughts race through my head. I would like to jump up thousands of miles to get away from here, from killing. Before, I did not know what it was like to kill a man; now that I have seen it, I don't want to do it any more. But it is the duty of a soldier to die for his country, me for our fatherland, the enemy for his. There is no choice."* (Vietnam 1939–1975, Neil de Marco)

This diagram shows underground air raid tunnels built by the Vietcong.

Although soldiers may be fighting on different sides and for different causes, their feelings about war and killing are often the same.

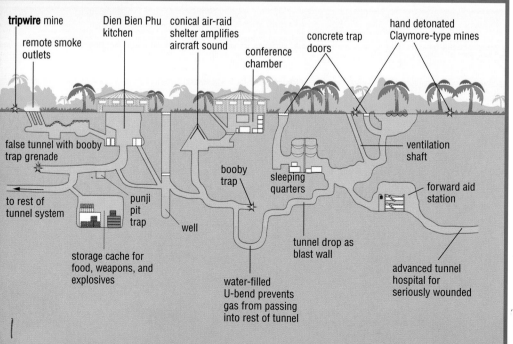

tripwire mine

remote smoke outlets

Dien Bien Phu kitchen

conical air-raid shelter amplifies aircraft sound

conference chamber

concrete trap doors

hand detonated Claymore-type mines

false tunnel with booby trap grenade

booby trap

sleeping quarters

ventilation shaft

forward aid station

to rest of tunnel system

punji pit trap

well

tunnel drop as blast wall

advanced tunnel hospital for seriously wounded

storage cache for food, weapons, and explosives

water-filled U-bend prevents gas from passing into rest of tunnel

Bombs and shelters

What the people of both North and South Vietnam feared most was being bombed by the Americans. Between 1964 and the end of 1971, 6.8 million tons (6.2 million tonnes) of bombs were dropped. This means 300 lbs (136 kg) of bombs for every man, woman, and child in Southeast Asia and 24 tons (22 tonnes) of bombs for every 640 acres (259 hectares). In many areas, huge craters covered the landscape. Around a million Vietnamese civilians were killed and there were 5 million **refugees.** To protect themselves from falling bombs, the Vietnamese people built underground tunnels where they could take shelter during attacks. The tunnels around Saigon stretched for 198 mi (320 km) and were well planned and constructed. Others were built quickly without much planning and were not always reliable.

These Vietnamese villagers are carrying children, burned by napalm, away from their burning village.

Phan Thi Kim Phuc (Kim)

In 1972, Phan Thi Kim Phuc (Kim) was nine years old. The Americans had ordered the South Vietnamese air force to attack her village, Trang Bang, with bombs and **napalm** because Vietcong guerrillas were hiding there. With others, she sheltered in the pagoda. The pagoda was hit. Two of Kim's brothers were among those killed. The terrified survivors ran onto the road where a U.S. photographer, Nick Ut, snapped them. The photograph became world-famous. It was named "Vietnam's Most Harrowing Photo" and awarded the **Pulitzer Prize.** The photo shows the terror and horror of war, and how very often innocent people can be drawn into war and be devastated by it. Kim survived the napalm attack. In 1996, she attended the annual Veterans Day Ceremony in Washington, D.C., and she is now a **UNESCO** Goodwill Ambassador. Her body still carries the scars left by the burns. She may have forgiven what happened but she will never be able to forget.

Photographer Vicki Goldberg was also at Trang Bang and later described what she saw:

The naked girl and the others ran toward us rather slowly, like people finishing their run. They passed the camera, it followed from behind. The girl's back and arm were seen to be completely covered with black patches of burned skin, no longer resembling flesh. U.S. soldiers gave her a drink and poured water over her.

The Antiwar Movement

The protest movement against the Vietnam War, sometimes called the "peace movement," began shortly after the war started. It lasted into the 1970s. At its height, millions of people were involved. The Vietnam War divided Americans. It also deeply divided the United States's European allies. It often resulted in great bitterness between those who supported it and those who opposed it. In the end, the protest movement was an important factor in the American decision to leave Vietnam and in ending the war itself.

Early protests

The first protest against U.S. involvement in Vietnam took place in New York in 1963. It was organized by Thomas Cornell, a member of the Catholic Worker Movement. The following year, Cornell formed the Catholic Peace Fellowship with two priests, Daniel and Philip Berrigan. In 1964, 25,000 people attended a peace rally in Washington, D.C. Some of those marching were socialists and **communists** who supported North Vietnam, but most were **pacifists.** They opposed the war because they believed that war and killing were morally wrong. Such a person was David Dellinger. He visited North Vietnam and saw for himself the suffering inflicted on civilians by U.S. bombing, despite claims that only military and industrial targets were being hit. Pacifists were so sure that the war was wrong that in November 1965, one of them, a **Quaker** from Baltimore named Norman Morrison, set fire to himself in the street. A few weeks later two others followed him. This was done to gain publicity and to draw attention to their views.

The antiwar movement began with young people and students, but older people increasingly joined in. This is an antiwar rally in New York, 1967.

Students

Thousands of students across the United States became the most active protesters against the war. In 1965, more than 3,000 attended the first antiwar "teach-in" at the University of Michigan, sparking off 100 further teach-ins across the country. At these events, students refused to attend lectures and to leave their universities. Instead, they spent the time with their teachers discussing the war and their opposition to the U.S. involvement in it. As this grew, student protests increased. In April 1965, 20,000 people attended a rally at the Washington Monument organized by the group Students for a Democratic Society. By 1967, student protests were becoming less peaceful. Strikes and shouting at government speakers were common.

The anti-draft movement

There were widespread protests against the **draft** by thousands of young Americans and their supporters. In 1965, David Miller publicly burned his draft card and was sentenced to two and a half years in prison. In late 1966, there was an increase in anti-draft protests after Bruce Dancis, a student at Cornell University, destroyed his draft card and mailed the remains to his draft board. Cornell students formed the first "We Won't Go" group, followed by two dozen such groups on college campuses. Burning draft cards became a common scene throughout the country, but the government was determined to punish those refusing to fight. When Philip Berrigan and three others poured blood on service records in the Baltimore Customs House, they were sentenced to six years in prison.

By the end of 1969, 34,000 "draft dodgers" were wanted by the police; and between 1963 and 1973, 9,118 men were prosecuted for avoiding it. In all, around 40,000 young Americans left the country to avoid the draft, 30,000 going to Canada. What really emphasized the horrors of the Vietnam War was the formation of "Vietnam Veterans Against the War" in 1967. This was a group of ex-soldiers who had fought in Vietnam and who were campaigning for the end of the U.S. involvement. They were given great publicity, particularly those disabled from injuries received in combat. They had seen the war first hand and were now completely opposed to it.

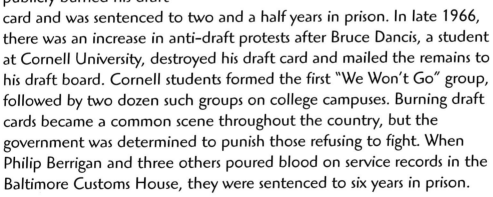

*Flowers were adapted as symbols of peace and love by the **"hippie"** culture of the 1960s. Here a demonstrator offers a flower to U.S. soldiers at an antiwar demonstration in Washington D.C., in 1967.*

Martin Luther King Jr.

In April 1967, around 400,000 attended a mass protest in New York City against the war. The protest included 175 young men who burned their **draft** cards. Present at the demonstration was the great African American civil rights leader, Martin Luther King Jr. King attacked the war, not only because he thought it was morally wrong, but also because the $66 million per day spent on it meant that the government had to cut back on programs to tackle poverty, especially among African Americans. Most of all, King objected to the number of African Americans fighting in Vietnam, when other young Americans, mostly white, at college, could avoid the draft. African Americans formed a larger percentage of the U.S. Army in Vietnam than they did in the U.S. population. African American militants wanted to go much further than King. They threatened to kill the whites who drafted them. In May 1967, the famous boxer, Muhammed Ali, was **indicted** for refusing to be drafted.

The march on the Pentagon

In 1967, 100,000 antiwar protesters gathered at the Lincoln Memorial in Washington. When the rally ended, more than 50,000 people marched to the **Pentagon,** the headquarters of the U.S. military, to continue their protest. The Pentagon was surrounded by 10,000 troops, armed with tear gas, clubs, and unloaded guns. When the protesters attempted to enter the building, violence broke out and 1,000 protesters were arrested. By the end of 1967, opposition to the war increased and became more violent.

Civil rights leader Martin Luther King Jr., attacked the Vietnam war.

1968—a terrible year for the United States

In the spring and early summer, Martin Luther King Jr., and Robert Kennedy, brother of former president John F. Kennedy, were assassinated. Although the killings were unconnected to the war, they were seen as terrible signs of increasing violence. The Tet Offensive in January 1968 surprised the U.S. military and made many realize the war could not be won. In a survey taken just after the Tet Offensive, 63 percent of Americans opposed the war. Protests against the war continued in the United States and throughout the world. Most capital cities in Western Europe saw violent demonstrations, particularly London and Paris. There were similar scenes in Australia. Soldiers from that country were fighting in Vietnam and there was strong opposition to their involvement. In the United States, the government decided to crack down heavily on protesters, particularly those encouraging young Americans to avoid the draft. Dr. Benjamin Spock, a famous expert and author on bringing up children, was indicted for draft-dodging. However, there were also parades supporting the war, often organized by World War II veterans' organizations.

Rioting occurred at the 1968 Democratic Convention when the police and antiwar protesters clashed.

Johnson decides to stand down

On March 31, 1968, worn down by the growing opposition to the war, Lyndon Johnson announced that he would not be running again for the U.S. presidency. Robert McNamara, the U.S. Defense Secretary, also announced his decision to retire. The antiwar movement saw Democratic senator Eugene McCarthy as the man to follow Johnson. In Chicago in August, the Democratic Party would meet to select their candidate to run for the presidency against Republican Richard Nixon.

Chicago 1968—the Democratic Party Convention

About 5,000 protesters arrived in Chicago at the time of the convention to protest against the war and to support McCarthy. Chicago's Mayor, Richard J. Daley, was ready for them. A total of 26,000 police, soldiers, and National Guardsmen had been assembled to protect the convention. On Wednesday afternoon, when Vice-President Hubert Humphrey was to be nominated as Democratic candidate, there were riots in Grant Park. Most protesters remained peaceful. Then they made their way to the Hilton Hotel, where the convention was taking place. The protesters were met by police and many were tear-gassed and clubbed. The beatings were filmed by television cameras and broadcast throughout the United States. Opinion polls later showed that most Americans supported the police action, including many who opposed the war. Seven protesters were later tried for conspiracy to start a riot. Five were found guilty but their sentences were overturned after they appealed the verdict.

Nixon and Continuing Protest

In January 1969, Richard Nixon was sworn in as U.S. president, promising to achieve in Vietnam "peace with honor." He wished to see an end to the war and troops coming home—but not just yet. Negotiations might be taking place in Geneva, Switzerland, to end the war but the Americans would stay in Vietnam until the South Vietnamese were able to fight the **Vietcong** themselves. Protests against the war continued. Huge marches took place in 1969 and 1970. In April 1971, around 500,000 people led by "Vietnam Veterans Against the War" took part in a protest in Washington, D.C. Two weeks later, only 15,000 took part in a demonstration in favor of the war. While Nixon seemed to be promising an eventual end to the fighting, the war appeared to be escalating, or getting worse. In March 1969, he ordered the secret bombing of Cambodia, although this was totally against international law. He bombed Cambodia because the Vietcong were using it as a base to attack South Vietnam. Yet in June he announced the first withdrawals of U.S. troops.

In 1970, four students were killed by National Guard troops during a demonstration at Kent State University, in Ohio.

Kent State University— May 1970

In April 1970, Nixon announced that U.S. troops had entered Cambodia to destroy **communist** bases used by the Vietcong. Protests took place in universities throughout the United States. On May 4 at Kent State University in Ohio, National Guardsmen opened fire on protesting students, killing four and injuring nine. The whole country was shocked by what had happened. The killings sparked off 400 protests and strikes in universities across the country.

Revelations about the "Phoenix Program"

In 1971, information was released about the work of the Central Intelligence Agency **(CIA)** in the Vietnam War. In 1967, they set up the "Phoenix Program." Its purpose was to identify and arrest Vietcong suspects in areas controlled by the South Vietnamese. The target was 3,000 suspects each month. The aim was to arrest them, get them to give information, and then put them in prison. Between 1968 and 1972, 28,000 Vietcong suspects were captured and imprisoned. Another 20,000 were assassinated and 17,000 changed sides. The program was effective and many communist bases were wiped out, but the methods were very controversial.

> High-ranking U.S. military officials were beginning to question the government's policies and tactics in Vietnam as well. Several U.S. Air Force generals risked court-martials to protect their men from the complex and often puzzling ROE set up by politicians.
>
> *America lost her first war ever because bureaucrats 10,000 miles away from the fighting played a kind of "war monopoly" game, in which stakes were not play money, but the lives of men sent out to die in the rice paddies and skies of Vietnam. Called to testify in a civil suit after the war, [Secretary of Defense Robert Strange] McNamara said under oath that he had decided as early as December 1965 that "the war could not be won militarily."*
>
> "Testing the Rules of Engagement" Joe Patrick

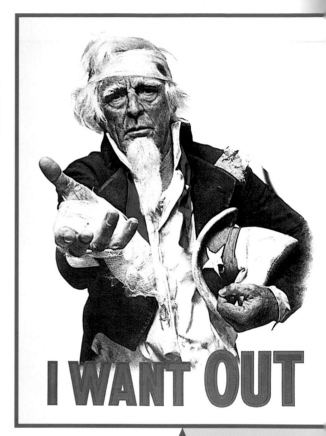

This is an antiwar poster. "Uncle Sam" had been used to recruit soldiers when the United States entered World War I in 1917.

Daniel Ellsberg and the Pentagon Papers

Daniel Ellsberg was a government employee who worked at the **Pentagon.** In 1967, he was asked to collect all documents relating to Vietnam since 1940. There were 4,000 pages. Ellsberg and others added another 3,000 pages of analysis. Together, they became known as the "Pentagon Papers." The documents showed that government officials had often lied about or covered up incidents in the war. Ellsberg, who had become an opponent of the war, photocopied the documents and released them to the *New York Times.* They began to be published in 1971. Nixon attempted to stop publication and to prosecute Ellsberg for theft and conspiracy. The U.S. Supreme Court ruled that the publication of the papers was not illegal and all charges against Ellsberg were dropped. The papers revealed a great deal about what had happened in Vietnam which had been kept secret from the U.S. people. It damaged the reputation of many involved in the war and strengthened the demands for peace.

Nixon: Vietnamization and Peace

Richard Nixon, president of the United States from 1969 to 1974, introduced the policy of Vietnamization.

Richard Milhous Nixon (1913–1994)

Richard Nixon's family were **Quakers.** They ran a citrus farm in California. He studied law at Duke University, in North Carolina. In 1942, during World War II, he became an officer in the U.S. Navy. When the war ended, he entered politics as a Republican, sat in Congress between 1946 and 1950 and then served as a senator until 1952. Between 1953 and 1961, Nixon was Eisenhower's vice-president. Nixon supported America's **Cold War** stand against **communism.** In 1960, Nixon ran for president against Democrat John F. Kennedy, but was defeated. He withdrew from national politics, but returned in 1968 as Republican candidate for president. He narrowly defeated Democrat Hubert Humphrey. Nixon set out to end the Vietnam War and improve relations with the communists. In 1972, he visited Beijing, China, in February and Moscow, Russia, in May. In 1972, Nixon was re-elected by a landslide, or overwhelming majority. His second term as president was dominated by scandals, of which Watergate was the most important. On August 9, 1974, he became the first ever U.S. president to be forced to resign. He died in 1994.

Nixon was elected President in 1968 mainly because he promised to "de-Americanize" the war. U.S. troops would slowly be brought home, but the war would go on until "peace with honor" had been won. For this, a policy of "Vietnamization" would be followed. The soldiers of the South Vietnamese Army would have to take over the fighting. The Americans would train and equip them but eventually pull out. Most important of all, the U.S. Air Force would continue to support South Vietnam and would bomb the North and other targets, if necessary.

Peace talks

In May 1968, peace talks between the United States and North Vietnam began in Paris. After one year, no progress had been made. The North Vietnamese wanted the whole of Vietnam to be reunited, but the

Americans wanted North and South to remain separate. North Vietnam wanted the communist **NLF** to be part of the new government in the south but the Americans wanted North Vietnamese and U.S. troops to leave South Vietnam, followed by free elections. Nixon believed that bombing the North would make them accept peace. He was wrong.

A peace agreement

By October 1972, a peace agreement had been worked out between the United States and North Vietnam, four and a half years after negotiations had begun. The chief North Vietnamese negotiator was Le Duc Tho. Henry Kissinger represented the United States. The terms of the peace agreement stated that

- All fighting throughout Indochina would stop.
- U.S. troops would withdraw from Vietnam within 60 days of the end of the fighting.
- U.S. prisoners of war, about 700, would be freed.
- Elections would be held in the South to choose a new government.
- Each side would stay only in those areas it controlled when the fighting stopped.

Henry Kissinger, U.S. Secretary of State from 1973 to 1976, was awarded the Nobel Peace prize in 1973 for his efforts to end the Vietnam War.

Nguyen Van Thieu, the South Vietnamese president, was furious at these terms. He realized that South Vietnam would be at the mercy of the North. But Kissinger was anxious for an agreement to be signed. The U.S. presidential elections were due in November. If the war could finally be ended, Nixon was certain to win the election. When Van Thieu rejected the agreement, North Vietnam broke off negotiations. On December 18, 1972, Nixon ordered another massive bombing of North Vietnam. The North started negotiations again and Van Thieu was forced to accept the agreement. It was signed in Paris on January 27, 1973.

The Americans withdraw

In April 1969, the number of U.S. troops in Vietnam was 484,330. In June, Nixon announced the withdrawal of 25,000 troops and a further 35,000 in September. By the end of 1971, only 158,000 remained. At the end of March 1973, the remaining 691 U.S. prisoners in North Vietnam were released. The last U.S. troops left Saigon on March 29, 1973. For most Americans, the Vietnam War was over, but not for the South Vietnamese.

The Collapse of South Vietnam

In early 1973, as the Americans were leaving, South Vietnam appeared to be in a strong position. It had the world's fourth largest air force and an army of one million soldiers equipped with modern U.S. weapons. The government of South Vietnam controlled 75 percent of the country and 85 percent of the people. The **communists,** on the other hand, were in a weak position. They were short of men, weapons, ammunition, and food. During 1973, the southern forces won victories in the fighting on the Cambodia border. The North Vietnamese and **Vietcong** forces were struggling to avoid defeat. The situation changed dramatically, however, and the army of South Vietnam soon began to collapse. By summer 1974, 90 percent of South Vietnamese soldiers were not being paid enough to support their families. Government officials were stealing their pay and the soldiers were threatening the peasants for money.

The fall of Saigon

When the North Vietnamese and Vietcong forces moved further south, the South Vietnamese could not stop them. By late spring 1975, Saigon was surrounded. Van Thieu complained that the Americans had let the South down, yet it still had plenty of guns and tanks. What it lacked was organization and leadership. On April 25, 1975, Van Thieu fled South Vietnam with hundreds of government officials. They were all frightened that when the communists took over, they would be captured, tortured, or even killed.

Nguyen Van Thieu became president of South Vietnam in 1967.

These U.S. troops are boarding a plane to leave Saigon in March 1973.

On April 30, the last 6,000 Americans to leave Vietnam were lifted out by helicopter. Thousands of Vietnamese civilians who had worked for the Americans also wanted to leave. They, too, were frightened about what would happen to them when the communists arrived. Unfortunately, there was not enough room left on the helicopters or other transportation leaving Saigon.

Panic set in as people fought for what places remained. On the same day, North Vietnamese and Vietcong soldiers entered Saigon. A tank broke down the gates of the presidential palace. The communists marched in. For all the people of Vietnam, the war was over.

The death toll

About two and a half million men, women, and children were killed as a result of the war. Of these, 900,000 were North Vietnamese and Vietcong soldiers, 223,000 were **ARVN** troops from South Vietnam, and about a million were civilians, many simply were caught up in the fighting by accident. U.S. military losses were 58,000, together with Australians and New Zealanders. The people of Vietnam and those of the United States were now about to start counting the cost in a variety of other ways.

Vietnamese Suffering

Of the millions who were harmed or damaged by the Vietnam War, it was the ordinary Vietnamese who suffered most. According to Ha Van Lau, a **communist** officer, there was "at least one dead, or some wounded in each Vietnamese family." It is estimated that in 1975, in South Vietnam alone, there were one million widows. Around 800,000 children had been orphaned or abandoned, some fathered by U.S. soldiers.

Damage and destruction

Heavy bombing of both North and South left widespread damage and destruction. Buildings, roads, railways, and bridges were destroyed and would have to be repaired before life could return to normal. The use of **herbicides** such as **"Agent Orange"** laid waste to large areas of forests and crops. Sixty percent of rubber plantations, 148,200 acres (60,000 hectares) of **mangrove** forests and millions of acres (hectares) of farm land were destroyed. Thousands of farm animals had been killed. Virtually all stocks of oil and gas had been wiped out as a result of the bombing. Because so much farmland had been destroyed, many Vietnamese faced starvation and disease.

This picture shows the horrible birth defects caused by exposure to Agent Orange.

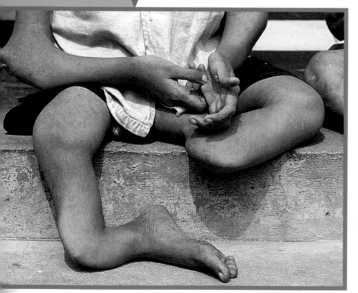

When the war ended, large amounts of weapons, including unexploded bombs and booby traps were left undiscovered. These could kill civilians who might not know what they were. Herbicides and chemicals had long-term effects. After the war, many who had been exposed to them began to develop cancers. Their children suffered birth deformities. Even today, thousands of deformed children are growing up in Vietnam as a result of such chemicals as "Agent Orange."

Reconstruction

Once the war ended, Vietnam became a united country under the communists. A huge task of reconstruction began. The country was desperately short of raw materials, and the wreckage of tanks and airplanes was used to rebuild factories and schools. All land was taken over by the government and farmers had to work on **collective farms.** The new communist government took over more than 500 factories in the South, producing textiles, chemicals, paper, and foods. Heavy industry, such as iron and steel, was given priority. But there was no money to spend on rebuilding industry in the badly-damaged country. Reconstruction had to depend on gifts and loans from other countries. More than 100 nations including Sweden, Australia, and the Soviet Union, which had broken off relations with Vietnam during the war restored them. All these countries provided money to help the rebuilding. The United States did not restore relations with Vietnam and provided no money. Vietnam remained a very poor country for many years to come.

Reeducation

Vietnam was now a communist country, and a program of **reeducation** began. About 200,000 senior military officers and soldiers from South Vietnam were placed in camps where they worked all day and in the evenings were given instruction in communist theory and obedience to the government. Objectors were sent to the "discipline house" where they were chained for many months, not permitted to see daylight, and threatened with starvation. Many died, and by 1983 there were still 63,000 in prison.

Refugees

As in most wars, after the fighting stopped, **refugees** became a serious problem. So much of the farming land had been destroyed that many left the countryside for the cities, especially Saigon, which was renamed Ho Chi Minh City. Many in the North were attracted to what appeared to be a better lifestyle there. In 1975, about 230,000 South Vietnamese left the country to settle in the United States and Canada. This number increased in 1978 after the Vietnamese government introduced laws against Chinese residents. Thousands of Chinese and Vietnamese refugees left Vietnam in crowded ships. Photographs of the "boat people" left a lasting impression throughout the world.

"Boat people" from Vietnam set sail in tiny, leaky boats to try to find a better life elsewhere.

The United States and the Vietnam War

For millions of Americans, whether they were directly or indirectly involved, the Vietnam War was a terrible experience. It lasted for twelve long years and was the first major war in U.S. history which the Americans lost. When the war finally came to an end in 1975, Americans began to count the cost in many different ways.

The financial cost

The Vietnam War cost the United States more than $120 billion. Even for the richest country in the world, this was a large amount. Most important of all, it meant that programs aimed to tackle social problems had to be postponed. Plans to clear city slums, to provide medical care for the poor, and to reduce racial inequality could not be carried out because the money was needed to pay for the cost of the Vietnam War. Abandoning these plans caused considerable bitterness and anger in the United States. Many questioned whether the war was really necessary.

The United States did not intervene when Soviet troops invaded Afghanistan in 1979.

The Vietnam Syndrome

The United States paid a heavy price in human suffering in Vietnam. The war left many Americans dead or injured. As a result, many began to question whether the United States should continue to get involved in fighting in other countries even if it was for "freedom and democracy." The Truman Doctrine seemed to be replaced by the Nixon Doctrine, which appeared to state that U.S. troops should only be sent into a country if the United States was directly threatened. This change in policy was a direct result of experiences in Vietnam—the Vietnam Syndrome. When Soviet Union troops invaded Afghanistan in 1979, the Americans did little or nothing to stop them. By 1991, however, this approach changed again when the United States went to war against Iraq for invading Kuwait.

When one returning U.S. soldier entered an airport bar, he was asked,
"How do you feel about killing all those innocent people?"
When he later offered to buy those in the bar a drink, he was bluntly told,
"We don't accept drinks from killers."
(*Vietnam 1939–1975*, Neil de Marco)

> The majority of Americans who fought in Vietnam performed their jobs and served with honor and dignity, and with a clear purpose.
>
> *We fought, not for a dream that was unobtainable, but for the idea of democracy, we fought against Communist aggression and for the type of life that we honestly believed in.... If we failed, it was not because we did not do our duty, it was because others entrusted with higher responsibilities failed to do theirs.*
>
> U.S. Vietnam verteran, 1999

Experiences of veterans

U.S. soldiers paid a heavy price for their involvement in Vietnam. Many who returned home when the war ended wondered what they had been fighting for. They had gone to Vietnam to support the South in the fight against **communism.** They had returned defeated, and angry that more than 58,000 of their comrades had been killed and more than 304,000 wounded. Those who fought in Vietnam and survived expected a warm welcome when they returned. They were often bitterly disappointed. A few were even treated as criminals and murderers by fellow Americans. Medical treatment for the wounded and disabled was not always of a good standard and they found it hard to get jobs, despite laws giving them priority. The **Returned and Services League** did not always provide much assistance in finding work. Veterans who found it difficult to settle into civilian life felt betrayed by the country they had fought for. Those who had fought in Vietnam clearly had a different view of the war from many members of the U.S. public. A public opinion poll taken in 1990 showed that 57 percent of Americans thought that it had been wrong to get involved in Vietnam, but 58 percent of veterans thought it had been right.

The film Born on the Fourth of July *told the story of disabled Vietnam war veterans protesting the poor medical treatment they were receiving.*

Some soldiers who fought in Vietnam suffered not only physical injury, but psychological damage as well. They experienced "post-traumatic stress disorder," as a result of fighting in the jungles and seeing their fellow soldiers killed. To many it brought depression and attacks of rage. Some found their marriages ending in divorce, others turned to drugs and alcohol. Suicide among ex-soldiers increased.

Changing Public Opinion

In most wars, public attitudes towards the fighting change dramatically during its course. This was certainly true of the United States during the Vietnam conflict. When the war began, most Americans supported it. The movie *The Green Berets* was made during the early years of the conflict. The U.S. Army controlled the script and it starred John Wayne. The message of the film was clear. The Americans were wholly good, fighting for freedom, and democracy. The **Vietcong** were wholly bad, fighting to destroy freedom and spread **communism.** This message seemed in tune with the thinking of the U.S. people at that time. As the war continued, there was a change in public opinion. As more U.S. soldiers were killed, opposition to the war grew. Films such as *The Deer Hunter* (1978), *Apocalyspe Now* (1979), *Platoon* (1986), *Full Metal Jacket* (1987), and *Hamburger Hill* (1987) gave a more honest view. So brutally realistic and depressing were some of the scenes in *Platoon,* that its director, Oliver Stone, a Vietnam veteran himself, had difficulty finding a studio to make it. By the time the film *Born on the Fourth of July* (1989) appeared, highlighting the life of disabled veteran Ron Kovic, the public had accepted more viewpoints about the war.

The Veterans' War Memorial

In November 1982, the veterans who fought in Vietnam were finally given a national memorial in Washington, D.C. Why did it take so long for a memorial to appear? The answer is complex. Perhaps Americans were not ready to honor those who had died so soon after the war ended. Perhaps there was still a strong sense of guilt about what had happened in Vietnam.

On November 13, 1982, 150,000 people assembled in Washington to witness the unveiling of the memorial to those who had died in Vietnam. It was the biggest crowd to assemble there since the funeral of President John F. Kennedy. The veterans marched down

This is the Vietnam Veteran's Memorial, a granite wall showing the names of all U.S. soldiers killed in Vietnam. It is in Washington, D.C.

Constitution Avenue to the memorial. Listed on the wall were the names of 58,132 men and eight women who died in the fighting. Also recorded are the names of 2,413 others, who have been listed as "Missing in Action." Thousands strained to touch the names of the dead.

Joel Swerdlow, a newspaper reporter later wrote: *All afternoon, all night, the next day and the next and the next for an unbroken stream of months and years, millions of Americans have come and experienced that frozen moment. The names have power, a life, all of their own. Even on the coldest days, sunlight makes them warm to the touch . . . Perhaps by touching, people renew their faith in love and in life, or perhaps they better understand sacrifice and sorrow. 'We're with you,' they say. 'We will never forget.'*

These Australian veterans are marching in the ANZAC day parade in Adelaide, Australia.

In Australia, Vietnam veterans led the march to remember ANZAC Day in 1987, and in October of the same year, a "Welcome Home March" was held in the federal capital, Sydney. In 1992, in Canberra, the Prime Minister, Paul Keating, unveiled The Australian Vietnam Forces National Memorial. In both Australia and the United States, the two national war memorials commemorate those who died in one of the worst 20th-century conflicts since the end of World War II. Those who survived had finally seen their dead comrades remembered in an honorable and dignified way. They could now try and get on with the rest of their lives.

Vietnam Timeline

1868   Vietnam becomes part of the French empire.

1890   Birth of Ho Chi Minh.

1930   Ho Chi Minh helps to form **Communist** Party in Indochina.

1940   Japan takes over Indochina.

1941   Ho Chi Minh forms **Vietminh** to fight the Japanese.

1945   Japan hands over power to the Vietminh and surrenders to the United States. Ho Chi Minh becomes president of Vietnam. French troops arrive in Vietnam.

1946   War breaks out between France and the Vietminh.

1949   Communist victory in China.

1954   France defeated at Dien Bien Phu. Geneva Agreement signed and French troops leave Vietnam.

1955   Ngo Dinh Diem becomes South Vietnamese president and orders the imprisonment of Vietminh suspects.

1957   Vietminh begin **guerrilla war** in South Vietnam.

1959   First U.S. military advisers killed in Vietnam.

1960   John F. Kennedy elected U.S. president. **NLF** formed.

1961   Kennedy promises more aid to South Vietnam.

1962   U.S. advisers in Vietnam increased from 700 to 12,000. "Strategic hamlet" policy begins.

1963   Buddhist protests against Diem begin—Buddhist monks commit suicide by setting fire to themselves. Diem killed in military takeover. President Kennedy assassinated in Dallas. Lyndon Johnson becomes president. 15,000 U.S. advisers in Vietnam.

1964   Congress passes Gulf of Tonkin Resolution. U.S. planes bomb North Vietnam and NLF attack U.S. air bases.

1965   Operation Rolling Thunder begins. First U.S. fighting troops sent to Vietnam, 184,310 U.S. troops in Vietnam.

1966   U.S. resumes bombing of North Vietnam. 385,300 U.S. troops in Vietnam.

1967   Van Thieu becomes South Vietnamese president. 485,600 U.S. troops in Vietnam.

1968   Tet Offensive. Major demonstrations in United States against the war. Massacre at My Lai. Johnson announces that he will not run for re-election. Peace talks begin in Paris. Richard Nixon elected U.S. president. 536,000 U.S. troops in Vietnam.

1969   Nixon begins Vietnamization program and announces troop withdrawals from Vietnam. Ho Chi Min dies in Hanoi. 484,330 U.S. troops in Vietnam.

1970 In demonstrations at Kent State University, four students killed. 335,790 U.S. troops in Vietnam.
1971 Lieutenant Calley convicted of My Lai massacre. 158,120 U.S. troops in Vietnam
1972 Nixon re-elected as president. 24,000 U.S. troops in Vietnam.
1973 Cease-fire signed in Paris. Last U.S. troops leave Vietnam.
1974 Nixon resigns over Watergate. Gerald Ford becomes president.
1975 Congress refuses to send U.S. troops to Vietnam. Van Thieu leaves Saigon for Taiwan. Saigon falls to NLF.

More Books to Read

Nonfiction

Gay, Kathlyn and Martin K. Gay. *Vietnam War*. Brookfield, Conn.: Twenty-First Century Books, Incorporated, 1996.

Isaacs, Sally Senzell. *America In the Time Of Martin Luther King, Jr.:1948–1976*. Chicago: Heinemann Library, 1999.

Myers, Walter Dean. *A Place Called Heartbreak: A Story of Vietnam*. Austin, Tex.: Raintree Steck-Vaughn Publishers, 1992.

Taylor, David. *The Cold War*. Chicago: Heinemann Library, 2001.

Wright, David. *Vietnam War*. Austin, Tex.: Raintree Steck-Vaughn Publishers, 1995.

Fiction

Antle, Nancy. *Touch Choices: A Story of the Vietnam War*. New York: Penguin Putnam Books for Young Readers, 1993.

Nelson, Theresa. *And One for All*. New York: Orchard Books, 1989.

Pevsner, Stella, and Fay Tang. *Sing for Your Father, Su Phan*. New York: Houghton Mifflin Company, 1997.

Glossary

Agent Orange most common defoliant used in the Vietnam War

amphetamine stimulant which acts on the central nervous system

anti-personnel bombs bombs containing plastic or steel needles that explode on impact and are designed to kill or injure people

ARVN Army of the Republic of Vietnam—South Vietnam's army

blockade to shut off an enemy area, such as a city or port, using troops or ships to stop supplies and messages from reaching the enemy

capitalism system which uses private wealth to produce goods

CIA (Central Intelligence Agency) U.S. government organization responsible for gathering and evaluating military, economic, and political information about other countries, much of it being classified or secret information

civil war war between different parties or groups within the same country

Cold War period of hostility and tension between two countries or power blocs which falls short of warfare

collective farms large farm or group of small farms organized and run by its workers, usually under a communist government control

communist follower of communism—a political system based on the idea that workers and peasants should control the country, its industry, and farms

dioxin chemical which can destroy the brain and central nervous system

domino theory Cold War theory held by many political leaders that proposes that if one country fell to communism then surrounding countries were likely to follow

draft in the United States, to force men into military service

grenade small explosive shell thrown by hand or shot from a rifle

guerrilla war type of warfare in which soldiers use "hit-and-run" tactics against the enemy. The word *guerrilla* comes from the Spanish word for "little war," and dates from the time between 1807 and 1814 when Spanish soldiers were fighting against Napoleon.

Gulf of Tonkin Resolution U.S. Congress Resolution of 1964 giving the president increased powers to conduct the Vietnam War

herbicide chemicals that destroy or reduce plant cover; used in Vietnam to kill jungle vegetation so that the Vietcong could not use it for cover

hippie 1960s term for an antiwar protester

indicted to have been officially charged with committing a crime

malaria infectious disease caused by a mosquito bite, characterized by fever and chills

mangrove tree that grows in muddy swamps or on tropical coasts

napalm jelly-like oil substance used in incendiary bombs

NLF (National Front for the Liberation of South Vietnam) political organization that fought for the uniting of South and North Vietnam

NVA North Vietnamese Army

pacifist person who believes that violence of any kind is unjustifiable and that one should not participate in war

pardoned to be officially cleared of a crime

Pentagon U.S. military headquarters near Washington, D.C.

platoon subdivision of a larger military unit

Pulitzer Prize one of a group of awards given annually to Americans for excellent work in music, journalism, history, and literature, named after newspaper owner, Joseph Pulitzer

Quaker member of the Society of Friends, a religious group that rejects war and stresses peace education

reeducation process by which thousands of Vietnamese were forcibly sent to camps to be instructed in communist theory and obedience to the government

refugees people forced to leave their homes and land, usually because of war

Returned and Services League organization of ex-soldiers who fought in Vietnam

trip-wire wire stretched close to the ground which, when touched, triggers an explosion

UNESCO agency of the United Nations that works to increase respect for human rights and fundamental freedoms for all people

Vietcong name used by Americans for the communist-led guerrilla army and political movement; officially known as the NLF

Vietminh organization founded by Ho Chi Minh to fight the French and Japanese to achieve independence for the Vietnamese people

Index